TENDER DATA

TENDER
DATA

MONICA McCLURE

BIRDS, LLC | AUSTIN, MINNEAPOLIS, NEW YORK, RALEIGH

Birds, LLC
Austin, Minneapolis, New York, Raleigh
www.birdsllc.com

Cover designed by Eric Amling
Cover art by Kim Keever
Interior designed by Michael Newton
Interior art by Emily Raw
Author photo by David Worthington
Glyph artwork by Monica McClure

Library of Congress Cataloging-in-Publication Data:
McClure, Monica
Tender Data/Monica McClure
Library of Congress Control Number: 2015934500

First Edition, 2015
ISBN-13: 978-0-9914298-2-0
Printed in the United States of America

Table of Contents

BLUE ANGEL

My Blue Angel comes to me
after the sanitation trucks

and asks
what drugs I need

Her finger waves are waxen
and her cupid's bow is stamped on

I say I want to be so sped up
my jaw swells shut

my body becomes negligible
and the world purely a dimension
peopled with bilious gestures

All modes of desire are simulated anyway

So don't feed me any duds
about poems
not being dialogical

Because I know a poem
by how much it does or does not
sound like its precursors

I don't actually need to feel anything at all
except that I live on an undulating plane
among artists

It's a middle ether of baby's breath and sprigs
of little cuntfaces under violet lights

and I do expect to be applauded
if I say this with aplomb

So can you please
give me a compliment today
starting with *you are*

You are not much of a caretaker

Blue Angel of unctuous balm

I don't know why I try
my charlatan captives at your desk
and talk to you about intellectual things

Blue Angel
you're like a worldly older girl
who took me on spring break
and locked me in a tower

with a Real World cast member

Why do we still use the language
of Feudalism

on the internet
An icon

Blue Angel remember

You are to be a well-uttered fuck
that disrupts my desire for coherence

I am unifying my affects
and privileging none

I want to be a woman!
Do I have to be
Yes

Radha waiting for Krishna in the garden
The bridegroom waiting for Christ

In these walls of my serfdom I wait half-dosed
ladling cream into my lap

In a civilization that has lost its purpose
I try to think of metaphor
as a paradoxical truth

I believe in beauty

If metaphor is truth
and truth is beauty

then I'm a Christian

Ok I wouldn't call myself a thinker
But I feel this world is wrong

has been from the beginning
Since the underground was made dirty
and the sky throne erected

This is why Bataille gave us the Acephale
Cut off the head to let the humors
hose through

The female passions unplugged from
their social vocation

and sprayed at the heavens like
scared animal piss

Probably wasn't Collette's idea
to sleep with the enemy

Yet when everything is possible we must
think of death as the first stop
on the way to online immortality

What if all my thoughts are deferred action
My girl lover Blue Angel

I didn't like when she tucked a pink Carnation
in my mailbox

I hate men
So why would I date someone who acts
like one

All the destruction caused by these
little castrated monsters
makes you think

Who is picking up the pieces

Women
are the only human beings

You Blue Angel of pharmaceuticals
have gone wrong too

For a very long time
you have led sheep to slaughter

hooking rising starlets in your cane
and dragging them out of vaudeville for good

Rub your acrid powder
on my gums

I'm moulting on the trapeze bar
while you make
my decisions

All season I've been
rehearsing in my sequins

while the other carnies have gone
to rural Italy
in the wagon of a muscular sadist

17th century blue
You are offering me chicken
feathers for wings

So I may taste the zeal
in my throat when I fall
and break my neck
in front of a million men marching

I can't say I don't deserve it

One Christmas morning
I woke up wearing
a belly chain restraint

A woman was singing
about black lacquered coffins
and then art came like a concussed champion

Art, who?
You asked for his last name

Blue Angel
I'm a natural nurturer

So if you won't take care of me
I will make you my infant

A shaman said if I hate myself I can't
believe in happiness

but I disagree

Oh transcendentalists
at the organic farm

happiness is not a condition
It's a calling

Go into big oil
Get the most out of life

Eagle Ford was like literally an ocean
under our feet

My Blue Angel
you poisoned me with false hope

Because I must inherit a role
you can put me underneath whoever

I'll respect the privacy
of our patrons

and someday
the lords will share their kingdom

I am not entitled to protection
No I have to earn it

I was given a child
as a "karmic learning lesson"

in need versus desire
for all I know

Now I finally feel
as if I deserve nothing

I force my utility upon
this tiny babe

Nipples and introductions
to the symbolic order

This is important

He grew into a boy
with bad vision
and grotesque bone structure

He checked payphones for change
and pick-pocketed the poor

As a crooked twenty-something
he joined ALEC

took my money and never
gave me tax advice

Long ago in the village we would
build up those around us

That's where I'm coming from

I built a treehouse of palm fronds for junkies
but he's not like me

Do I regard him narcissistically
this child who regards me
narcissistically

Wow so terrible to bleed and not die
like some hunter's chimera

I'm haunted again
by girlhood hallucinations

The black bull who walked on two legs
pacing the porch

Blue Angel
come back and
take the edge off

To the extent that I did not become
the black bull with red eyes
I became a woman

Judith Butler my son castrates me
on an imaginary schedule
I hate him

Men can't structurally see women
We loom like shadowy shrieks
in the entrance

the way Euripides wanted it

My child takes the gentle on all fours

You angel of order
give me back the lethargy
my tourniquet of blue

The meek are not born

Their cars are
wrecked repossessed impounded

Objects of desire and identification
repeatedly lost and recovered

This is the dark side of environmentalism

You punish it for leaving
But there really are

no exits
Nothing is extinguished

Ann Coulter Phyllis Schlafly
you will sit at the children's table
in heaven

Richard II you wish
your name could be blotted out

Such a social thing to say
Did you ever think of anal rape by a bull

or reading fiction to feel
more like yourself

Blue Angel
You were right to explode
this shit show

into drama

LUXE INTERIORITY

I was starved for love
Now I've just had an abortion
It's Mercedes Benz Fashion Week
but I don't want to go to the shows
The social worker who performed
my intake consultation had lined
her eyes with Kohl's
I think I would like to be a part of culture
while remaining without
Michel Foucault says
there is no such thing as outside
But that's exactly
where I need this thing to be
Lack, you are my lackey bitch
A bean does not become a stalk
that I may genuflect in its monument
I refuse to be stuffed full of myth
when I can live like a blade on ice
W Magazine at the Minor Emergency Center
How common some names
I study the wedding photos
of Margaux Hemingway and Bernard Fauchier
On a poor girl her brows would look unkempt
I see only what I know to be baroque
The white patio furniture hot from the sun
immolating and free from function
The receptionist screams, "I'm a crazy witch!"
and I'm so startled I throw up my Valium
Why should "I" be in Massachusetts
scared shitless by the subjectivity of regular folks
their paranoid existences
when I could be getting photographed
in a nude bodysuit in a white room
But if that's what she wants to put out there, ok

DEAD SOULS

Religious men will try to tell you
that every abortion is special
and to some extent I agree
I was inconsolable when I missed prom
and had to pay a woman to pretend
to be my mother so I could
obtain parental consent
Every citizen of this world is on trial
I'm learning to speak legalese
as I stroll through civil law like
a gamine through a sample sale
Kendra said she knew a doctor
who would perform abortions for minors
as long as you didn't tear up
during the ultrasound
I looked all over Houston for him
getting fatter and richer as I went
This all could have been avoided if I'd
convinced an over-18-year-old
to sell me her birth control
if my mother wasn't a Christian
and if the nurse hadn't insisted that Kendra
swallow the morning after pill
in front of her as I waited
in the parking lot of T.J. Maxx
It wasn't my prom exactly
I was a freshman invited by
my upper-class boyfriend
Gulp your items down
the nurse said
If there's one thing I've learned
from watching *Snapped* it's don't
be a woman on trial
Outside the clinic
my poverty makes me brash
Now that I'm free I can go
to the Diane Von Furstenberg party

sponsored by Veuve Cliquot
in droll Easthampton
I'm not a wise man
I'm too fertile for that
But I can tell you that some abortions
are more convenient than others
and I've taken notes on how not to
be a poor soul

PRIVATE EYES

Although I am adulterous it had never occurred to me
to live a secret celibate life
I'm going to
All relationships are libidinal let's be honest
Even good men are assholes
Mine is an asshole
Do I care? I wonder
This poem is wasteful of the darkness
allotted for it
As long as I'm getting these sexts
I've got only one hand
Sometimes art has to be like that too
Off-kilter but dipping deep
from the public center

BEAUTY SCHOOL DROPOUT

I want to solve the problem of heterosexual desire
like why do I love dick so much
Is there something transcendent about self-abasement
I'm not a licensed esthetician so
I don't know what scholars say
about Brazilian Keratin Treatments
The formaldehyde stylists breathe is Adam's Curse
To be a woman is to know one must starve
I don't feel very straight at all
I masturbate to underground gay thug porn
and still wind up thinking
about the male gaze
how without taste it is
I want to be so skinny people ask if I'm dying
Have you ever been on the roof of The Standard
and noticed your tatters
in the unforgiving sun
What do the stewards check for
in the bathrooms when they walk
into your stall after you exit
Is it unicorn piss if it's your
sappy inner monologue
There is a guy here who looks like an heir
and every woman here would sleep with him
except for me

PALE BLUES

I want to write in my journal
ballads about how my boyfriend left me
for a more cosmopolitan woman
but that's never happened
for no woman is more worldly than I
only more complementary
My last abortion bled
the darkness out of me
Something about the warmth of the sheets
in the St. Tropez clinic
and how the doctor smelled like lime verbena
Or was it my second day tan

ADDERALL

I would do addy over cocaine any day
Let's take a long ride on the A train snorting
orange crush time release beads
This older man I dated
called it his performance enhancer
When he went to lecture at a Rabbinical school in LA
he let me stay in his Park Slope brownstone
Thank G-d he approved of abortions
I felt bad for blowing a guy on his futon
during the carnival scene of *The Third Man*
I'm too young to manage a full-time sugar daddy
I never saw an amphetamine I didn't like
Why should I be stuck with this
gentile mental capacity
I weigh the powder on a balance
Already I feel it tipping in my favor
I've never met a worse poor person than myself
I didn't avoid pregnancy and county jail
to sound like George W. Bush
I reject a language manipulated by folklore
and white people watching ESPN
I want to live in a kingdom of style and camp
I want to relate this smut to Vienna after the war
When finally those who really got glamour
despite their transience and poverty
with just a little industriousness could live
like movie stars in the bombed out rubble
Jean Rhys up to her dimples
in black market velvet and meringue
the chartreuse clouds hanging in the death sky
It'll never be this good for her again
There's a child in the orphanage who needs money

OLIVE JUICE

The Plan B pill fizzed when I dropped it
in my dirty martini
I needed to relax at The Carlyle
after breaking down on the subway
When the price of birth control went up
I got so pregnant
I had to drop out of SCAD
which was a shame because I was
absorbing the delicate Spirit of History
The son of a corrupt billionaire art collector hick
roofied my green PBR
at a St. Patty's Day party in Normal, Illinois
Now I have to go to Ibiza
to get my hymen repaired
before the Daughters of the Revolution find out
Surgeons never believe this nose is mine
because it's perfect
Anglican like a Boston Brahmin's
If you're interested in laughing succeeding
and making memories with fun-loving people
you can be in any club you want
I want to ignore the dominant aesthetic
of my time so I've tried living
in places where only ad campaigns reach me
I fear I am going to die
a very plain death
in the county where I was born
Djuna and Jean both lived to be 94
after countless heartbreaks
in foreign cities

BAKHTIN

I used to want to be safe but now
all I want is to be twirled in the palm
of a Victorian maître d' at Marea
That is I want to be poured into a form
like a capitalist epic
taking place in the full light of the
historical novelistic day
Everyone will say she wanted to study
a language that had just been born
but she was no great skimmer of culture
She was not online
Well not in the right ways
Put your hands together and pray for us
was her feeble thematic throughway

JELLIES

If he only knew how many times I took Plan B
because of him he would text me:
"Good morning, love pot. The world is real
and verisimilar. I believe in love as something
outside of consciousness subject to study like germs.
Thus, I also believe in God and magic."
I'm looking to rent the runway tonight
because I need to look happy
at this art opening
so I can post my image
to the feed inside his eyelids
If only my menses didn't get everywhere
I'm down to my period panties
Can we have a girly day at La Perla
This woman he's dating is like so old
I hope she breaks her hip trying
to take pictures of her legs for her tumblr
She is Blanche Dubois and the internet
is her low-lit yellow room
I'm glad these associations come easily
mitigating my despair
Peplum is back in muted colors
but I want something in lime green latex
Maybe when I lose five pounds after this abortion
I'll wear a leotard with some mist over it
How intertextual I grow
I will twist my silk turban in a bow
I wrote to Ford Madox Ford for money
but he's been dead forever

I DON'T LIKE YOU

If we were fighting over a baby
I would just let you keep it
so the stress of parenting would age you
And I would get drunk
on Diet Coke grenadine and vodka
and show up at the baptism
with the only man who ever
broke your heart
I want you to feel like cutting
and then I want you to feel nothing at all
All my life I've grasped for a raft
on the Sargasso Sea of my moods
I amputate myself and conceal
the cast offs in a pouch
When I was threatened with a stint
in juvy I rolled a sandwich bag of weed
and worked it inside myself
Could your lover come over and help me
feel like I'm of use to mankind
There's a knife under my fainting couch
that I'll use to chop off your passé bangs
I pondered the scuff marks
on my Louboutins but couldn't focus
without stimulants
on what to do about it
You are pretty I admit
with the right Instagram filter
inverting the ontological relationship
of beauty and time
like this faded Nashville
the name of the city where I bled myself
into a flute of Dom Perignon
until it turned pink in the glow
of the La Quinta Inn lampshade
I don't know you really at all

But I compare our social media profiles
every single day
Fashion and the digital don't function in opposition
We must ask ourselves only
how good or how bad is it

JACKING

No one would suspect a pregnant woman
if she was strolling a toddler
with white lobster buried under its blanket
I pulled a few Winonas in the early 2000s
because I was angry and hungry
In a fit of remorse I threw those gowns away
the ones I wore under my cape and maxi skirt
as I strolled out of Valentino
The puce sequined backless number
I got impregnated in by the most handsome
of the 1,113 Saudi princes
is the one I miss most of all
In the penthouse of the Four Seasons
there was a view of 2012 like you wouldn't believe
I threw money at a bridgeable gap and cabbed
to the next year's rented room
The perimeter was lined with oiled
Italian men's shoes
For this memory to make sense
there must be a gap in perception
an interruption
like "wtf how did I get here?"
There is unity in heterogeneity
like I know I am only what I'm not
I left the $5000 he offered me
for sex on the floor
I'm more like one big whaaaaaat
I have a roster of actresses
that I could at any given moment
choose to play me
How do I explain interpellation
to men wearing jerseys
What fools what fools
and yet I want their cross-eyed disdain
Men they're so unlike me
I love their idea of becoming themselves

HOUSE OF JOYCE LESLIE

If I could be anything
I would be a rich white girl
and I am almost halfway there
I straightened my hair before it rained
Now all I can do is pray
I don't mean that figuratively
I'm living in this logocentrism
Where did I get these Spanish thighs
I was crying in the food court
because I'm afraid
of the spiritual anorexia that I crave
I wrote out a prayer in reportorial style
like a good Protestant
Obsessed with achieving
the androgyny of my time
I cut when my boyfriend said
I had the figure
of an average Hispanic girl
so what was I so upset about
I decided to try liposuction at home
So much splendor is owed
to dysmorphia and a fucked perspective
like those Gothic spires poking the heavens
that someone just thought up like
can we tap this broomstick
on ethereal marble floors or what
can we really do

GIRLS ROOM

I've always lacked volition
I could never choose one over another
I'm self-taught at being liked
so I don't have to choose who to like
There's so much affection in me to give
to the person I pity the most
A woman once told me
that she'd always been intact
Her femininity was a perfect seashell
wearing red cowgirl boots
and dragging a feather boa on the ground
I'm skeptical but not altogether
ruling it out
I can't read the signs fast enough
so I don't drive my own car
When I'm with a man I feel
like a gay man
When I'm with a woman I feel
like a gay man who is into women
And I only feel truly fabulous
in the presence
of someone less girly
This is my romance with gender
I play it with semiotic excess
in long seasons
I silent act and forget sometimes
to come out

BIRACIAL BARTENDER

If you dropped your birth control pill
on the floor
I would step on it
I don't like your ambiguous class status
Are you the rich daughter of multinational
corporations or are you
an antebellum mutt
They say you're exotic looking
but you just look confusing to me
like someone from an obscure island
You said my Asian girlfriend looked robotic
and it's ok
You were just being honest
It's hard to see human expression
on the faces of those more divine
Where is the sire to my seedling
I haven't seen him since he broke a chair
across my threshold
I don't care if he's violent
Red bone yellow bone muscle and bone
A freakish relic of postmodernity
like a white girl with a black girl's ass
or a straight male poet
who said he fucked his first
colored girl and didn't
use a condom
To be political one must simply be
awake when the half-breed
denies his white patriarch
Sweet clerk of milk-grey skin
Color swatches breed ideologies
Willa Cather's bloomers becoming disturbed
when she writes of ochre landscapes

I'm not making this stuff up
Milton did when he wrote
of utter pandemonium
In general I do hate all straight men
Specifically I think they're unnecessary
Pantone of my years
My chalice of Creole rum

HEY DICK

You don't get to say how I look
more Mexican when my hair is curly
or that my Korean friend looks bored
or that I can't have your baby
or that I should get vaginal rejuvenation
or that hope is stupid
or that nobody likes you
or that you wish you'd never been born
or that John Locke ran around getting things right
or that you believe in nothing but love
or that I'm dead in the near dystopic future
or that the wind whistles songs through my teeth
or that my name is in the word harmonica
or how you awoke in a field with dew on your lids
or how you built a house and burned it down
or how you took me to an island and buried me in fire ants
or that you're good at anything
or that women think you're good at anything
or that you'll lower my heart into an empty well
or that the eschaton will arrive trumpeting gospel
or that crickets coax music out of heat
or that you want to be buried in my garter belt
or how sex is so intense when you're hungover
or how you said oh my god aloud ten times
or that you'll hang yourself with a chain of daisies
Because I'm tired of it
and I could get pregnant at any moment
from sheer desire and biology
and the frailty of my intentions
and the science of causality
over which I will squat and pee
I have no reciprocity with time
I'm retreating into the art directed life
and leaving you on the floor of the self-cutting room
It's got its own special kind of misery

OPPORTUNITY COSTS

When I'm having trouble conceptualizing
for pseudo-intellectuals at the party
I'm only mimicking
the psychic structures I'm describing
The women at the dry bar
are having their oils blasted
by the hands of strangers
The window is a fascist city unto itself
All you need for a movie is a camera
with an open aperture
There are two reasons a woman
goes to the dry bar at lunch
a date or a job interview
How appallingly self-preservative of them
I want someone like me
And what is something I want besides
something I want to have
I created a prize
to be accepted tonight at Cipriani
for Exemplary Humanitarian Service Despite
Her Internationally Fluent Attractiveness
She's been pursued by hegemony
from such a tender age
but chose to forgo the more lucrative choice
Now she is at the dry bar
a subject invented and surveilled
with the precise heat on her scalp
and my gaze pushing speculum inside
I sat through all five hours of Faust
Then I cried from Times Square to Brooklyn
wearing the wrong outfit
When I got home
I laid inside a circle of batteries
and masturbated myself to sleep
after my boyfriend passed out drunk
in another apartment
The next day he dumped me on gchat
for being secretive

WHITE GIRL WASTED

There's nothing inherently noble about work
At New York Dolls I could choose to sit
and let men buy my drinks
instead of hauling ice buckets
of champagne across the mainstage floor
I didn't make money when I got drunk
instead of getting men drunk
but I was not cold or sober either
My heels dangled from the bar stool
as I watched the engorged breasts of girls
tremble in the arcade-like wavelengths
weightless and bovine
A happy couple stumbled in and soon
the wife was throwing up
in our dressing room
We held her hair back
careful not to drop ashes
in her shiny blowout
I was Kathy Acker in the 80s
doing nothing exceptional yet everything
in a corset without muscles
Her husband had paid for two hours upstairs
and was up to his watches in flesh
You girls are mistaken I said
to seduce this stupid city
Then I went home no richer or poorer
than when I showed up
I wish I could get shit-faced wasted
on my own dime
and have someone I trust carry
me screaming and drooling into a taxi
I think of the words of Anastasia
the fat ballerina of the Bolshoi
"I'm going to fuck the shit out of this world."
Goodnight swans on your lakes of vodka

ASH BLONDES

When she asked me what kind
of girls I liked
I told her as honestly as I could
that I wanted a fair-haired woman
like Catherine Deneuve
whose skin is chlorinated
and repulsive to her own sight
I like when she's on the swim team
and dizzying a tub of wormwood oil
with her reed-like fingers
It's always been obvious to me
that an object-choice is
an object-identification too
I should have tried to become smart
Above my bed my name fills
glass tubes of absinthe bowed in an "M"
If she were a Christian Creationist I could
live for a while in the fortress of her
If she were saving herself for her husband
I would think that is the most
coquettish thing
She said "So you basically like...me?"
I kissed her on a mattress of hot pink
and touched her virginal mouth
with my whole hand
I don't want to fetishize purity
I want to understand her
one woman to another
But like any man I can't help myself

MONICA MCCLURE

Monica, vain as two crystals in a window
Monica, proportionate face like a student drawing
Monica, passable body like a non-celebrity
Monica, competing affects getting crossed
Monica, languid like a tranquilizer napping in the sun
Monica, sensitive like an artist coming to terms with failure
Monica, signing over her paltry assets
Monica, sleazy like the nouveau riche
Monica, watching herself while watching you
Monica, like a summer in the shade of a factory
Monica, editorial like the ego ideal and like the ideal ego
Monica, effusive like alka seltzer
Monica, blushing like purple areola
Monica, disarming like a borderline
Monica, free as a stolen mink
Monica, steadfast as scotch from an Islay faraway
Monica, lost like a puppy in an undertow
Monica, like iambs in a cavern
Monica, like grey birds aerial diving
Monica, broken like tea leaves in the hand of Jack the Ripper
Monica, in love for the empire and courtly manners
Monica, menstruating with endless iron
Monica, like a truck full of hoop skirts
Monica, sculptural with Debuffet's dirty pick
Monica, saintly fallopian tubes butterflying
Monica, easy like a promise to make
Monica, sluggish as the mind in conversation with itself
Monica, kissing deep a plum cooled on mint

YOUR TRUE SEASON

Because urbanites can't look at mountains
we dress ourselves like birds of paradise
in falsies and teeter
on Alexander McQueen flamingos
clutching gold knuckles to our breasts
Bodice make me bold tonight and if I die
before I wake let this embryo inside me never take
hold of my uterine lining for my
24-inch waistline's sake
When I was a girl I would rip the yellow
OBGYN listings out of the phone book
and watch them sail on a river so refractive
I'd swear it wore French skincare products
The song of doves was prelapsarian
They answered each other always like
poor Echo in her cave
wailing "There is only subjective truth!"
which was a statement never heard before
repeated so many times it lost all its power
No body just the history of her libidinal choices
I had not thought to compare the ego
to a video game because I was so deep in it
I was all drives and instincts
This is why one should never try to explain
art with personal experience
Still I plan to take full control of the situation
by annihilating meaning
I lost my virginity on a fence post
I lost it to my middle finger
And I was like a balloon full of saline
when I straddled a balance beam
This is how I lost it
like a circus girl somersaulting
for the thrill of her inner spectator

NUDE IN THE CAT HOUSE

If you are slutty you will be reincarnated
as a rescue cat in a Las Vegas brothel
and you won't want to be sex positive anymore
but nonetheless you will rub and rub
yourself against the oiled thighs
of fruity desert angels
as they bow-drill money out of cocks
And if you try to be moral you will be
reincarnated as a dog
and you will learn next time
not to go in for morality (in Edie Bouvier voice)
Olympia with your taut body refusing
to slouch or arch or grow plump
whose maid is presenting that bouquet to you
and where did you hide your own paintings
Jean Paul Gaultier's pieces are difficult
to take off in a hurry and yet
I've managed to eek out a living
and to find comfort with a scholar
who is gentle and fluent in wine
We sometimes walk through Rouen
while the soprano voices of children's choirs
sanctify our routines our humanistic pursuits
We've styled our lives after Pinterests of modest leisure
I may have failed to be one type of artist
but I am with the professor I adore
inside the only realist novel I'll ever write

CLOWN ROOM

In all earnestness I built an altar
to the saint of lost ephemera
because he's the only gentleman
on whom I've ever been able to count
though he performs a useless duty
by preserving a glut of sentiments
I wish there was such a thing as
deleting your landfill
Sometimes I miss a chivalrous doctrine
I want to be a crusader with a train
of pious courtesans
In the sensual eastern sun
pitch me a silk tent
along the unfaithed road
I am in the playpen of someone else's god
with torture toys that confound me
I tried to pee while standing up
and wet the lace of my petticoat
It's this revelry that truly rescues me
Seriously the only thing
worth staying sober for today

FLASHDANCERS

If someone says poetess
I am going to scream and chop
a hobby horse to pieces
with an axe
I try to understand those women
part mother substitute
part broken pair of wings

MAMMARY

The Chateau Marmont in winter
is like a beautiful woman in the morning
on the second day of her period
It's a body rejecting its implants
Lindsay Lohan is walking around
like she owes the place
sliding into the darkest seat
with two lesbian truckers
I'm sipping an Italian aperitif
and feeling exuberant
like it's the 20th century
and a love sick Breton is whispering
messages on my answering machine
in an empty antechamber
while I check my powder on my iPhone
When I lost my academic job
I became an unskilled sex worker
and got pregnant out of professional frustration
My mother drove me to a midwife
in the first light of morning
Lazy Susans on the table spin me
another cold highball

BLACK WIDOW

My hometown has one stoplight and it's me
wearing opera gloves
on a gravel backroad
Centuries ago I burned myself
as a witch on this
very fence post which still stands
I refuse to be barbaric
Now I'm back here to repent
I'm sorry I didn't get pregnant
with a dead man's child
My dear townspeople
that would have been difficult
to bear gracefully
My life would have become
all gravity and the suckling
love of an enemy
I want some fetishist to buy these
white knee socks in my Amazon wishlist
I don't like to think of my origins
the fairy flags splattered in blood
alliances made from the exchange of women
a decade of childbirth
Before I succumbed to suicide I grabbed
the numb wrists of men
and made their fingers to rub
like teething toys
ineffectually over my clit
Charmed I'm sure to meet me again
in this graceful iteration
I've kicked pretty high on these platforms
I'm sure

CLASS SONG

If I were a man I would turn this
self-violence onto you
The lace was still gathered at my throat
when they collected my bones
among embers and opal
But haven't you heard we rise
from the ashes with our red hair
It's too bad I dreamed of Cambridge
but couldn't get accepted
because of two Class B misdemeanors
I wanted to be among great men
Monica hearts Philip Larkin 4evah

VACUUM

That doesn't sound so bad
One big suck and you're back
to the races again
looking for careers
trying to get hired based on merits
expensive receipts from universities
I don't want to learn how to play the game
because I might embarrass myself
I told the bankers who shared their cocaine
at the Polo match
that money bored me
They said "But you look good, like you do care."
I castrated them with horsewhips
pulling the knot till their circulation slowed
like a live wire dying
and laid down repentantly beside them
as the night regularly bled over our heads
Torture was not even my idea
In fact it was yours
But it's ok gentlemen
There are tart bubbles in my nose
and the clitoris commands a mighty army
of pleasure soldiers
I turn to other stories
Josephine Baker walking her tiger
through the Champs Elysees
Djuna's mail from home
her grandmother's drawings
of her own saggy breasts
leaking milk from the ache
of intellectual abandonment
I wanted to be one hell of a shop girl
and became a chorus girl instead
I walked around in the dresses of wives
fashioned myself into brass
and never once got in the family way

SCREEN GRAB

Stay focused and you'll stay alive
But if you don't survive
people will still jack off to your
Facebook pictures when your
corpse is siphoning black soil
through its Geisha mouth
What is it like to age out of sexual arousal
things to write Southern Gothic novels about
Be inspired by the internet
or become irrelevant overnight
The slick death of menses
Styrofoam cups in New Orleans
I want to live a slow and humid life
Beauty has been cruel to me
By the time I could afford a vanity
my face had lost its petal

OLD NEWS

I want babies to clamor at my breasts
to become pregnant while I'm young
and to expose my buttermilk
nipples to screaming mouths
I want to be a teen mom
skinny arms around my huge bump
My need for narrative arc will lead me to believe
that everything happens for a reason
mandated by some globally rich
third-world princess
upon whose mercy I depend
I see her as clearly as I see myself
posing on a plush rug
with her bleached skin
sheep heads mounted above the bed
crying real tears into ivory vases
I watch my little girl's dance recital
I tell her she too must wait
for her look to come into vogue

CANDY FLIPPING

I'll miss coming home and kissing
my twinks when the work
of twinks falls out
of parlance
when we grow paunches
I walked past the Nuyorican Poets Cafe
for the first time
after taking off my clothes for
a mannerly photographer
He must not see many
girls with an ass like this
He asked "Can I say something sexist?"
I could hear the echoes of woo girls
outside of last night's bars
When owls say woo
during the daytime
your bad luck ends there
and doom takes over
This is the end of your family line
Across the border rainbow flags tatter
The mothers wearing clogs
push listlessly against the willows
their babies woo
I did something poetic today
when I faced the wall
and let him fire rapid shots
He was famous in the 80s
I don't want to be an incubator
for meaning
I want to stick to the membrane
and make some money
before the white owl curses my last beads

FUNNY MONEY

Someday I'll be a nectarine girl
wearing a sari at Ethnic Appreciation Day
where I have been invited
to induct the International Day of Happiness
and pose for a picture with Colin Powell
I'm sure I will like pink faces doused in fake cum
I'll get on my knees for war criminals
and music producers
What is best for my little earthlings
is best for my conscience
I don't regret accepting money
in exchange for healing love acts
Eros has her own currency
Some people say I should be a model
or an Indie queen
But all I really want
is to live a beautiful life
paid for by someone who feels
indebted to manhood
For him I will fill the bathtub
with expensive rosewater
that I got for free in press swag bags
I'll stuff holes with pure sugarcane
bought with the IMF budget of countries
who failed to understand the compromising
nature of relationships
On this special day I encourage you
to keep track of how many songs
you get per lap dance

FROM EPIC TO LYRIC

Your insides make you
who you are
I think of my womb
It's like a landscape from a Beckett play
You can adorn yourself with euphemisms
but underneath there is an unrepresentable truth
All you want is to express yourself
through fashion
like a canary racking itself
against a barn
The eyes of axolotls have no lids
no interest in the conceal-reveal trick
of good style
Psychology makes me truly a woman
What subject could invent
itself and presume
to be monitored in this aridity
Burroughs moved to Kansas
to get used to no one caring
when he died
Production is not creation
the latter requiring almost no work
When the carnival left town
I always felt robbed
of an obscure cure
whose secret is intentionally
protected by its stigma
I'm only cut out for childbearing
Who am I speaking to
through this monoglossic headset
I honestly don't know
So I let myself get pregnant
by a wealthy Presbyterian minister geneticist

When you decide to live
for someone else
it's so mature
like having your own stash of coke
and doing it moderately
to get ideas for your screenplay
How can I talk like this?
In this unconscious language
that was a language to begin with
I have bigger things to worry about
than being authentic
I looked in the mirror

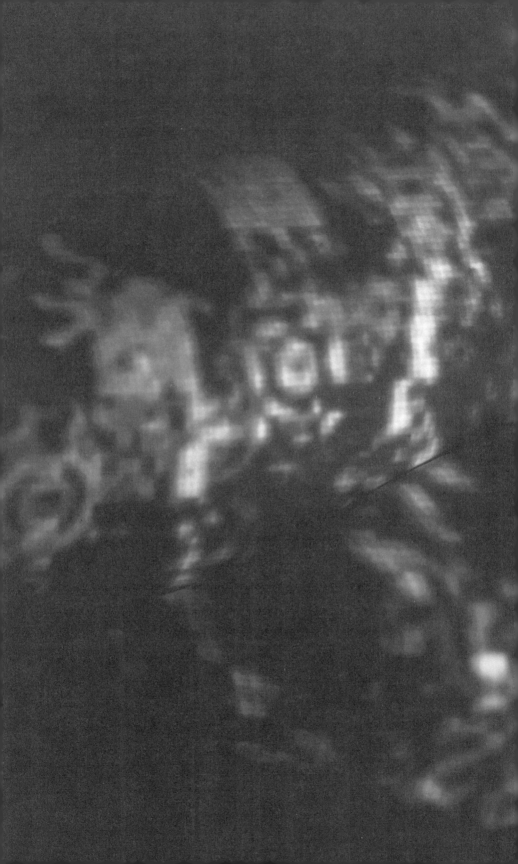

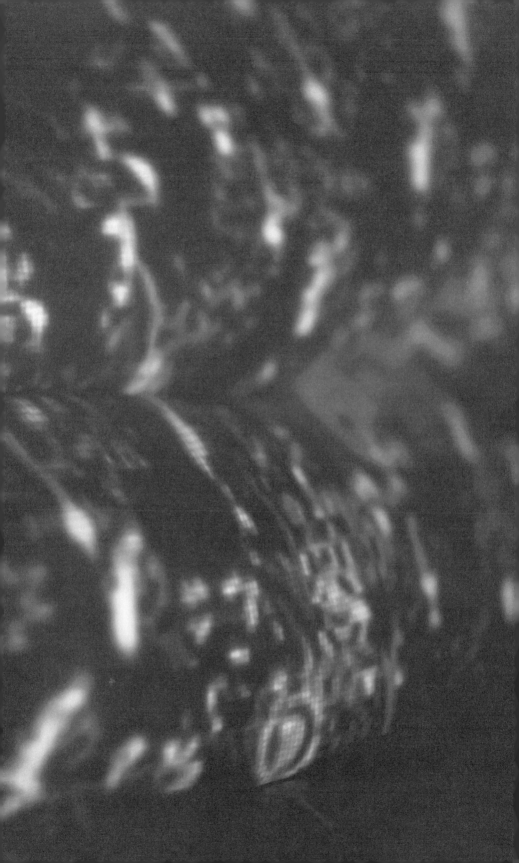

TENDER DATA

Inquiries feel like enemas
What is it called when your fist blooms
inside someone

The civilization I live in has lost its purpose

so I turn to amateur porn

Because I long to believe that people hide
deeper truths in their genitals

reality slicked
down with spit-wet lace

Invisible panty lines and IUDs
Instrumental promises of the soul's efficacy
to carry you past the threshold

of shame
The entrance to the cervix

opening once a month like the doors of Jubilee
We genuflect to use value

Another day bustling around
Mrs. Dalloway's foyer

And the river clearly runs through it
to a crevice in your body
I can't follow

Look away you profane
who would conceal from me
the stable reality within
its gilded domes of meaning

I want cruelty turned inside out
Blood out flesh in
a glass of divinity sending rainbows
shot with plagues
ungodlike

The question of evil
turns raspy in the throat of my ego
gawds gawds gawds of no
pale ankles

gawds of
You don't have the guts for me
Why people do evil is
the only question worth asking

Dear deity of I am standing above a pit where bodies
quit their living like thunder in a pile

and my handsome mark says
"It's really beautiful here. I don't know what to
do with that."

While gathering mushrooms into a small bouquet
a girl from a town of burning pyres is born

I am a composition of absence so heavy
I call it Marlene Dietrich

That a man would not recognize
the limitlessness of my nudity is hard to accept

for the greatest sexual experience of my life
happened in a room pasted with
pictures of my lover's dead fiancé

Because I laid a trap to catch his trauma
with my sad sap

That is my favorite
word for my body
My A plan

Plan B
Put as much in
your head as possible
before the coming wars

I had wanted our grieving to be stickier
I thought it would stay inside
with my Marxism
and our lazy America

I could lead a country one day
for all I know
It's not up to me

All the women I'm not
line up to bring me diamond cuffs
because they don't have the guts for me

I could take a monogrammed gold
pair of scissors to mine
but no one's made weapons from my name yet

I could become the women I am not
but I can't forgive myself

for disappointing a civilization
designed to give me rights
as long as I fulfill simple responsibilities

I may straddle the two Os
in the HOLLYWOOD sign
and jump

Low verb highway
History's continual drug-addled orgasm

I love acting beyond repair
and branding my damage

A deer twists on the curb
and a rose grows necrotic with overdraft fees
Some ideologies are only party girls in decay

Don't pick me up again
Oh sacrament boy returned from Afghanistan
to tell me my art is waste

When enough's enough
I want to dignify it with my body

to fold my hands
over my holes
and hold the waste inside
like a spirit

Rights without responsibilities—
that's the kind of humanism I want

One day you will look into my swampy green irises
heavily lined with blue
and give me health insurance

Why should the transnationals get the goods
when we are swimming sickly
in the black water with the cold eels squirming
in our veins

Below the yachts
where their perfume
turns over a new warm layer

Everyone let your eels out
Let them convulse through marble corridors
as golf courses burn

Maybe it's shame that will finally deliver me
I found panties stained with his ex-girlfriend's period blood
and put them on

I can sell you my secret
for unlimited access to your Adderall prescription

Sometimes life is like
dating a rapper who is afraid of
hard drugs

I privately sneered at you
the whole time

Taboo will take us through the red curtains
Shame and poetry
I return to you

What shouldn't be
flayed for the king's entertainment

What isn't false that can't be stripped
I knew a Teuton from Chicago who thought a fallacious
person was a criminal

pinned disgracefully on those who peep-show
at the game's finest moment

Look earnestly inside me for there is
a temple of mirrors

where the devout marry
Join me in these moments of evacuation because
I am a collection of your eyes

Behind this Chloe dress I hide a deep universal truth
A vintage scarf folded on the body

a coffin is rife
with non-Euclidean meaning

When you stop watching yourself
a spirit will come arrest us all

Even sacred cows find their butchers
inside a triangle of surveillance

the lover watching the beloved
being watched by the rival

My Abraham Darby backstage
watching the makeup emulsify

That's the kind of thing that siphons me out
viscous on the walls

of Roman catacombs evaporating on contact
with human voices of the past
hollow in their unthinkable meekness

The best words don't function
as language or function
at all

Like the way my leisure time is overdrawn
Words are there to stop us
from getting too intimate with continuity
and recognition

Can the heroes in heaven tell my cunt
from the cunts of others

My work whether I mean it or not
is defamiliarizing

Would you ever accept cookies from men
who approach you on the street
or would you assume they mean heroin

No thanks to my contemporaries
for the street smarts

This hot swill in the chest is mine
and so is he and so is she

I don't know how else to say this
There's nothing inside me
worth fighting over

If I'm too good to dance at this club
then go ahead and pull it out of me

I was in a pro-ana phase
when I was taken to the Body Worlds exhibit
on the South Side of Chicago

That's where I wrote the memoir of my carcass
her persistent desire

Because I was euphoric from starving
I was able to use the "I" to fuck the "I" out

until it trembled
and broke into stars about my spine

Then I took some Klonopin and threw up
and passed out

And when I opened my eyes he was
putting on his shoes
and taking me to a White Sox game

so proudly slumming it
with his well-insured pockets

and his watch
pointed like a laser on my back

not long after
he had called my family
white trash

Hello I'm brown on the inside
And if you look for my trash
you won't find it

though rest assured it is on me
like my masters' vistas
like my ancestors' crop

Working night shifts is like
trying to home remedy
a relentless yeast infection
with yogurt with garlic

Never the right appetite
at the appropriate time

The light is always getting mopped up
before it can bathe me
in optimism

Power is so cute when it tries
to hide its impotence

Consumer romances and the apparatuses
of micro-class are seesawing
across my reflective screens

Do I want to look good
Or do I want to look rich and if not rich protected
and if not protected coveted

Of course erotics troubles this line of reasoning
In the same way
an obscene picture of a stranger
even a fictional character

is dangerous
to the decency
of all the people you love

Hello Monica
Helloo Monica how are you today?
Hello Monica
Hello Monica, Milk of Milton —

Dead moments in a high-gloss shine
Djuna and her grandmother
Did they fuck?

The lack of irony in the middle ages
was not sexy
rather sexual

But then again I don't really know how peasants
approached the Bible

So when I read that radical mimesis is original sin
I think those serfs were better artists than any of us

We are orphaned birds who can't grow up
until we see our lost magnified selves

How to fill a father-space in the sky
with what enters us from our mother
through the heels

Carnivals still travel
Think of it
Their kitsch yet uncompromisingly sordid
arrival in a homogeneous town

Wearing brown scrubs with name tags
strangers in the grocery line
The erotic promise of nomadic life

On our way back from spring break in Florida
we shared our ultimate sexual fantasies

In the middle ages they wouldn't
have confused imitation with heresy

so we too reached
for the resemblances in our differences

in order to act on desire
in order to keep the farce alive

Laura liked to pretend it was her first year of marriage
and she was in the intercourse stage
of getting pregnant

A spring break Carnival cruise
Yes that's when I started to feel really gay

I skipped cocktails and went out to drown myself
There was a storm at sea

I had a copy of Jeanette Winterson's *Lighthousekeeping*
that I'd found in a Key West bookstore

You went to that bookstore too?
No wonder our sex is so swampy

You changed me slightly
in the summertime
I want to ask

How horny were you after she died
You can tell me I actually understand

I still crawl into his hospital bed
There is always an empty quarry
between us to cross

What has been emptied gets refilled
until we forget and the container dissolves

When real people expose themselves
can you enjoy it without giving them money?

When my earring fell on his forehead
was it erotic before he was dead?

I accidentally smoked crank once and couldn't
remember being born

I took this as proof that I didn't exist
and spent four hours in my dorm room
having labor-like contractions.

I've always said men go to strip clubs
to spend money in front of
other men

Sell your witnessing before it's sold to you first
Otherwise you can't be sure of your aptitude
for sight

I'm just glad I'm the first living girl to get you off
in four years
while the dead bear witness in their frames

Anything illicit excites
Nothing sanctioned does
So we tell secrets

Cordelia flirts with her father for the first half of *King Lear*
Then Bakhtin ignores Shakespeare altogether

I really would like to know what Bakhtin would say!
I know I'm high but really I am
religious that way

If I have so many more nerve endings
in my clit
than you have in your hand
why does it feel so bad for me and
so neutral for you

I rebirthed myself again
when it became clear that I had just
smoked ice
What does it mean to find self truths
in poison and poverty

The white powder turned rainbow-colored
in the foil boat

The migrant workers had left their candles
in a triangle on the floor

The one-room structure still functions as
a seasonal slave shanty
Many others have been adapted

as permanent homes and expanded
My relatives paint their walls different colors
every month to hide it

Our Lady of Fleas
Bless this barn in Ethiopia where you slept
with the goats
and looked to my nudes for solace

Give thanks
that the cotton disappeared in time

Women don't act like my gentlemen suitors
who fill me with disgust
and an all consuming desire to please

I feel chubby today
but smart
so it's kind of okay

That night I knew we were making personal history
My back was sweaty in the moonlight
Death was nearby

On your birthday the freeway sex store
will give you flavored lube

It's a special gimmick to mark
an eternally recurring moment of manufactured vice

Are lesbians into lighthouses
Is it a thing

PTSD in my very own bed
I feel like a hard journalist

After I traded anal sex
for your cooperation at the party

You told me about a particular dead man's brother
who seemed more human
because he was still wearing his sneakers

I believe in love
as an accumulative effect of these nights

Because we got really monstrous
to grieve accordingly for this world

We scraped off the shellac and
grow nettles

I left the scarf you brought from Tunisia
in a British pub on Macdougal

The loss pierced my hand
and was felt as a caress in Cairo
where you were squinting at a lens

Ambulatory as I silently wish you freedom
from my clawing
I believe I love you in the highest order
like a son

How I hope my nakedness serves you
when you're afraid

I asked you to tell me how she played volleyball
the way her ass looked on the beach
before she was killed

Let me explain to you how the deaths of lovers
change us
Are you fucked up
Do you see a shrink

The future when I didn't escape to New Orleans
is suspended at the tip of my lips
covered in sticky magic

If you google me you can find my body
fructified like literally

Life is not valuable everywhere
So there must be something beyond it
say the wrongheaded
who might be our prophets

I promise I'm not hiding anything inside my body
so I'm not very useful
as amateur pornography
or a hostage

It's all perceptible sometimes
There's no such thing as capitalism
with a human face

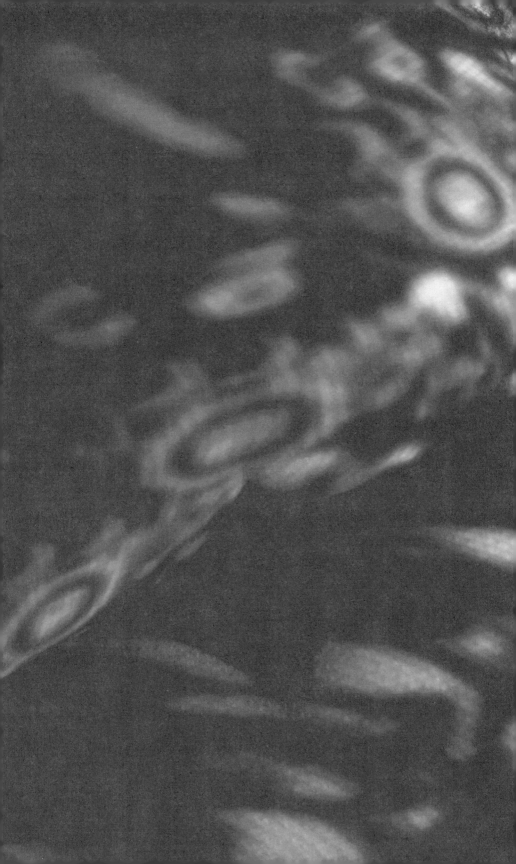

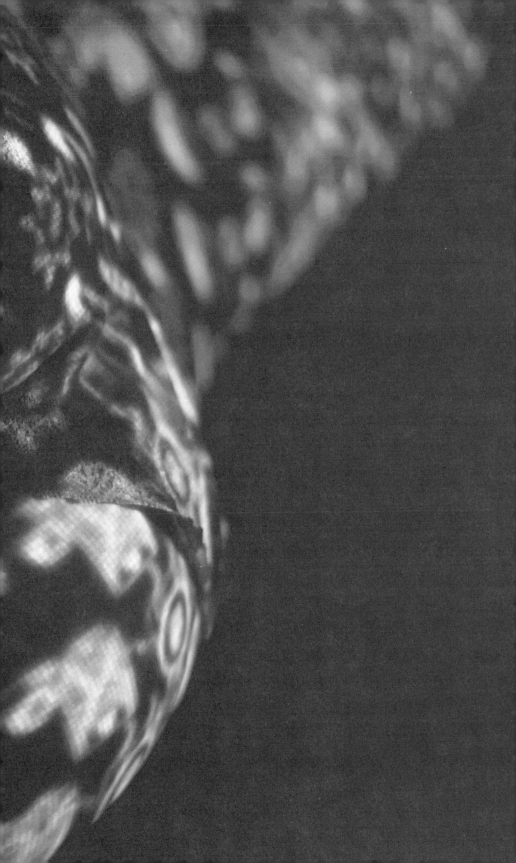

CHIFLADA

I typed a message that cost
ten cents to a guy who couldn't read
At the mall the vendors sold
translucent cases for chubby Motorolas

What was I supposed to say to a woman like her
For months the water was rationed
Horses rolled on their collicked bellies

My mother said don't look so scared
out in public
Why are you so chiflada with your
nails sticking in your teeth

I wanted mass cultural desire to prostrate
at my walls
mutant muñecas
in their configurations of play and discipline

I wanted Britney Spears' perfect midriff
my fingers slicing water shocked with tablets

My palms sought the contours
of a psychosocial muse

Not the handbag
but the Graces that eluded me

But instead of duende I got voluptuaries
lusty for wind chimes and frozen food

The bellybutton was the
erogenous zone of the early 2000s
a bronze bedknob of tween sexuality

It wasn't actually getting anyone off
only rubbing the undraped curtains
of their Blockbuster dreams

On the north side bare waists sloshed
through films of hair products swirling in the pool

Where the city controlled the power box
the projects lit up at curfew
extraterrestrial under lime green gels

It was a rumor industrial complex
based on quasi Christian media fantasies:

The abstinence of Britney Spears
and the allegiance of school shooters to Satan
of unlicensed day care centers to Satan
of Mexican citizens to ritual murder
of blue-eyed boys
for Satan

Thong underwear
neutered by its utility
The end of pantylines

Black lights vanish cellulite
and turn you smooth and brown

Something's got you covered
even fingers hanging
like tentacles from the lower lip

Rhinestone Irish crosses
bubble wrapped
over push-up bras

She clicked her acrylic nails on the keys
and balanced her risks

To stabilize the costs of our choices the women
joined together in air-conditioned
rooms for civil gossip

I had to keep my head down
chiflada around people whose people
were invested in a localized history
its ineluctable modality of the folkloric

Given limited resources
the choice to bare full midriff
at whatever cost incurred was
so chiflada like who did I think I was

One minute Elvis
and the next a shrinking violet

I hadn't learned how to masturbate yet
but sometimes with my bladder full
I felt pressure

Chiflada alone for hours
turned inward like the eyes of the well-bred
looking demurely down
at their antebellum waistlines

The cops were sexual predators and
racists circling the projects
staring down the wall where
The White Front stood aslant

People said don't be so chiflada
with your boyfriend's mother

The boys sat on the walls and smoked blunts
dipped in embalming fluid
The girls went jacking in the town

I learned the two worst
things about county jail are
the lights that never go off
and disposable underwear

Lip gloss is meant to insinuate
that the wearer has just slobbered
over something too big
for her mouth

Glistening and fruity how
we took the Limited Too in
our JCPenney's bags all summer

However lethargic I was from pressing
my bladder into the cool springs
of my parents' mattress

However sore my ears from sleeping
on the phone the glow of *VH1*
pinkening the walls

In her ugly refurbished kitchen
with my shirt pulled down
I tried not to be chiflada when
she was saying

this man is making my panties wet
Tonight I'm bringing you home a new daddy

I didn't get how impoverished
opportunities can be
when you're acting chiflada
with the auctioneer

Feeling entitled to a solace of oneself
while the talkers take seats and
organize the festival parade

Turner Classic Movies with my hand
in my cheerleading shorts
as Deenie Loomis backs
into Bud's car
with her red bangles trembling
like toy cymbals

My boyfriend whose body
was scaffolded against feeling and
so more like a girl's body hairless
and so masochistically sunburned

I get that
I'm lacerated with passion
on the salon chairs at Suzie's Secrets
acting chiflada

the wrong way
In public I am silent and vain

My boyfriend's fathers
were washed up bull riders
One died in the kitchen
the other fondled his sister

But the in-ground pool
was blue salve
cool indemnity

Potions of amnesia swallowed
with chlorine and Hawaiian Punch
from her pointed pinky thimble

Town beauties who married
last year were widowed by now

How did they get so fat so fast

Her boss was paying
for the pool and
the cars in the driveway

I had maybe the cutest stomach
inflected enough to be well
gripped and lifted

I dreamt thick needles
passed through it like wet clay

There will be another luncheon
this year for the ladies of the town

Even the festival queens who
were stripped of their crowns for
getting pregnant unmarried
will sip lightly

Liqueurs of preservation taken
with the nose pinched and hair furled
in unironic foam rollers

She sat under the press box
a creation goddess drawing the sex
on her son's taut pelvis as we kneeled

in the brief infinities
of our nymphic fever youths

Teenage women crowded by her feet
but I was too good to say hi too chiflada
to make small talk

Because I worried about getting caught
under the heel of a passing epoch
that's all about Like Whatever and
talk to the ineffectual hand

Audre Lorde said shyness is shit
and she's right

The redneck aspiring bourgeoisie
is not breaking eye contact
anytime soon

One afternoon in the American Legion Hall
my Uncle Tommy was pointing at me saying
that little white girl over there
is my niece

And I got that too
The windowless dark the primeval smoke
of sausage and cigarettes where they
exposed their absurd prizes unashamed
to be with each other

while the canons squatted in the heat
like tired pickers and the chismosas lumbered
down the grocery aisles
making faces making eyes

But in the dark it wasn't chiflada

The vets unbuttoned their shirts
past their bellies and I was shown
how to rub the blue chalk over the cue
and take aim at the corners

Though I couldn't stop making faces
or quite sink into a soft water there
or so far anywhere

There is no such thing as
class without propriety

Decorum in lieu of ownership
is called putting on airs like
wearing white muslin to
eat tamales in a yard of dirt

Money buys time but no money buys nothing
but time and there was no relief from
the pressure that spread across my waistband

In the pool I swayed
with only their bodies
simple people so tractable
and unprofitably corrupt

The girls in their boy shorts
pretending to be pushed in

by the boys growing weedy
and more native
with every chemical splash

PETOCHA
an autohistoria-teoría

Virginity is $$$
in a vintage velvet pouch

Touch her if you can for virginity is
not real
but she is wanting
to be touched

I got ojo because they stared
at my virginity for pleasure
I was a child so they left me
untouched

My virginity is going to fall out sooner
than later
because I'm sin verguenza

Sana sana colita de rana
si no sanas hoy sanarás mañana

My aunt is rolling an egg
on my flat chest
which somehow aroused
pleasure

in someone who looked
but couldn't touch me
out of pleasure

because I'm too young for pleasure
and too chiflada

When you meet your boyfriend's family
don't be so chiflada with them
like you are with us
Why are you so chiflada with us?

Who looked at my bottom lip quivering
and wanted to touch it
but didn't

My hair is falling out because someone
wanted to pull my curls
but didn't

My whole body is sliding out
between my knees and everyone stares
making puchetos

Don't be so chiflada with your fingers
in your mouth all day

Ojo is what sickens you when they
want to touch what they see
and don't

because she's like puta madre
and racks herself on a bike crossbar
before it's tomorrow

I am sick again
Inside the house the babies
are making puchetos at me
I suck their fat cheeks til they squeal

Short of money your purity
makes you an object
of exchange
Mina Loy said get rid of it
as fast as you can

La Virgen de Guadalupe
said keep your sexual snakes
coiled below the earth

She was fifteen and bathed in light
when she blessed the Spanish
for their good fucking

Pa que se ponga chingon
Close your eyes and think
of your new country

which is your old country
seized twice because
they liked what they saw
and didn't kiss La Chingada
when they fucked her

What are you looking for
up on the roof tonta
My mother asks why I'm so chiflada
and pulls my chongita and slaps my mouth

Pobrecita
There is more time than this life
Now behold

I am the mother of Mexico
the Philippines
the whole pinche Americas

I am Patron Saint of Unborn Children
so put down your forceps and multiply
and starve in the desert
cabrones

The Mexican men say
their women only want
to get married so they're no fun

But I'm a petocha
that is
a girl with a lot of attitude
an international playgirl
a tomboy with a little purse
like a puta
for cigarettes and change

I'm sick
Can someone here touch me
if they want to

I need some witchcraft
and to meet a white man
who's richer than my father
the postero

A white man called a wood chopper
is little more than a hillbilly shitkicker

no manches
I don't want none of that

Some women have their hymens
sewn back together with her-pleasure
ribbing and lubrication

But men can tell with
their evil eyes

Sucias with their hair unwashed
and the chickens pecking
at their bare legs
in their short skirts

susias dancing
on their broken eggs
without shame

A petocha is a girl built for horseplay
They are mounted
on the wide Dutch shoulders of men
in the club

They're spitting in the cops' faces
and inciting the French girls to riot

And who doesn't want to live
without shame

I feel sick
like someone kicked me
between my legs

I feel chiflada
like I can't control my mood swings

A petocha is a shorty in a gang
with the bubbling eyes
of a nymphomaniac

She's protected by the men
that she out pisses as long as
she says yes yes yes yes yes yes yes yes yes
a huevo a huevo a huevo guey

They taught me to say no mames
and I love to say no mames
because even if you wanted to
suck me off you couldn't
I wouldn't let you

No mames is the first thing I say
when the world is on her knees
and I don't need to be blown

When a mob of hands
is saying hey guera linda

hey guera mala
hey hey reyna
que onda que pedo que o le
que chula que bonita que mal

wanting to suck me off
and I'm saying no mames

NACO

When the people in power are anti-civilization
and pro tribal

litigious over the void
standing bow-legged across the opening

where we hope to crawl up
and nurse our young

under the heat lamps
of their groins

and the sun is a private park benevolently opened
to the adequately employed public
Who are your people

I saw them bringing me soup
and putting their pierced tongues

in my mouth when I couldn't
fuck right in Spanish

Let the trucks pass by wailing of gas
sour morning song of nacos

I want to hold the dry weed of my people
inside me paranoid and mute

until the wet L.A. Looks
dries prickly on my bivalve body

I saw them freaking out in the cemetery last night
high as the afterlife

When Coca-Cola takes the water away will you bathe
in that viscous nectar you drink

I saw you sucking out our hangovers
through my clit
as half my guilty heart went mushy

You were letting your jeans get pliable
with unwash and bus seats for all
the gringas to scorn

My manners are beside the point if I don't use them
The people in the mountains aren't coming down
anytime soon

so what's the point of trying to look not naco
with a not naco polo shirt and not naco gold chains
not naco bone structure and not naco height

I'll tell my people a story about a Spaniard on
a white horse who fell in love at first sight
with our great great grandmothers

so that every generation after had indigenous lovers
of their own

in the pantry room in secret
and that's not rape cuz it's not even true

It's just a nice story about a stallion and the
emergence of the mestizo race

This naco showed up in the darkness to
choose me because my sister is cute but I am cuter
he said with eyes a lil limpid and evil still

because the exorcism didn't work
when he was a child

the people were so crazy
for Barbie dolls just like

all these city dogs hounding the hills
walking right up to my crotch
are crazy for plastic flesh to fang

After I die from slumming it
that'll be a good time to join the military
and take bribes

then do naco things all day
like snarl at the passing tanks of military excess

and kiss your mother wetly on the mouth
her red rosary scraping your chest

And I'll come naca as I am
to your sister's bed
even when it's covered in dolphin print
sheets and dry semen

because I saw you whistling to your mother's bird
and holding my hand on the traffic side hoping

to share my outlet malls of overflow and clean pussy
cuz I'm aspirational brands & tap water
fast food & bathroom attendants

Speaking English with the German boys
secretly ranchita
like a naco

I saw my people scooping
mayonnaise and chili into styrofoam cups
and calling me mutt

As trashy as the unfortunate position
that citizenship affords us with
all its surplus hygienics
and piety

Our children too will be naco
and they'll sit on shards of plastic chairs
and they'll chase starving goats with sticks

as our bass and accordions echo
macho in the spiritual mountains where
a deal was made long ago

to form a new tribe
and tell everyone else
to act civilized

MACHA

All my feelings are
different and this one
is the most

Of all places here
where women once retired
from the men for fear
of boring them

I am so bloody in my own bath
of wild hairs
that I couldn't possibly
join you tonight
for that colonial thing

Heroin or whore
Babylon or Bethlehem

No matter what I'm followed by
mosquitos

Flitting dicks who want me
to teach them about themselves

But everything I know is contained in capsules
of macha that break down
in my bloodstream

And I wouldn't recommend it
for the fairer sex
who should buck up and study up
on their condition

I used to feel sick for all my sloth
but not anymore

In wanting to please
I have sinned
In leaning in I have sinned

In breaking in two
I feel sin
So

Vete ya
A haircut and a hard cock
is all I need

To govern a family
My rod

cutting them down
supplicant on the ground

For I was the first real white girl ever born
in this country of flat skulls

That's why I'm so cocky
with my staff

and my rule rock hard and inconsistent
with my favor

The mouths of L'Age d'Or
suckled well at my pre-war stockings
before cocktail hour

Bells rang and trays of mosquitoes
were served with tarts

We hadn't meant to kill them with La Macha
which includes but is not limited to:

a goddess religion
unfaltering at the altar of shade
an erotics of object-identification
and compassion extending beyond the grave

My sister and I drank mournfully but afterwards
we still danced all night

wearing quite literally bedazzled bustiers
and veils of a dead boy's smoke

que mala after beating their macho dead
in ultra-feminine swoops

How do they want us to think of them now
our brothers having left so little charisma behind

on the internet
to aggrandize

Such small mosquitos
And though we are mourning we are still so macha

as we chip the thin teeth of traitors
and huff the scent of babies
and slap each other on the asses
and father seven times
and punish the bull
with its own marbled horns

But though we're cocky we are still martyrs
My sister says quita la macha
and I'm like why

It's ok to make up slogans in the spirit of revolution
and she's like ok but

after you systemically destroy machismo you must
put his teeth to gnash at your engorged breasts
for any sort of catagenesis to occur

and I'm like that could be hot
But it isn't the new love
conceived by and for macha

or is it?
idk
idk either
i really dk

So we taught our brothers all these methods of cameo
that they may take a small symbol of macha
to wear around their necks
to the part of culture where the money
used to be kept

May they remember the strength
of their mother's biceps as they show mercy
to their fathers who are teleological

till the end of supremacy
which is the beginning of macha

Kiss the black lips that feed you
the corn hips that rock you
and blight the prayers after you've said them

Santa Mala
Madre de Mala
ruega por nosotros pecadores
ahora y en la hora de nuestra muerte

Hand me my beads
War without end
Amén

MALA

I had a boyfriend named Angel de los Santos
Angel of the saints

Together we were Gabriel
set atop a marbled ogee craning in the old gym
towards a pure wing-brush

Never seen a winter before
Never had a Sistine feeling of ice-blue enlightenment

I think my mother was a child on this floor
when my archangel's big mouth proffered my buds

Now there's vaginal discharge and then there's children
I'm brown and yet my whiteness is laminate
making me a bright smear of a girl over wood

We were the angel Michael in gloss
on a bed of trumpeting whore babies

I loved my fear and nursed it

My xenophobic mums with jangles
My plastic cupid pussy
My hairless bedazzling machine missing parts
The homemade pillows of bad

My skin is a shuddering prig

When I'm beaten and starchy with my brown-out lust
When I don't like Latin men anymore

I had a girlfriend named Sara Finn
That's it that's all

In front of the band hall a black girl broke
a brown girl's
face on the pavement
The children would scream "Fight Fight
a Mexican and a White"
defining white by contrast

So the white girl's head
was crushed on the blacktop

She was my girlfriend
and her name was Selena Quintanilla-Perez

And she was brown
as gasoline on a roughneck's clothes

In a cool blue dressing room she buried me in hoops
sent from God to make the rhyme work

after I'd nearly been drowned by her friends
who were a gang of vulgar angels

jumped in by giants
holding my head under water
with their nephilim strength

in my hull hair
in my scared Indian blood

Wearing street clothes in the pool
Wearing wet parachute shirts and chains
Their billows my word and their billows

I was a prig in love with angels of saints and I was nothing
but what I wanted to transcend
I said things like my word

My girlfriend was named Cher Abin
That's it that's all
I loved my tailless cat and nursed it

When my blood was rusty it was Indian blood
and it pumped for hemophiliacs on CMT

It gurgled for Fancy's poor cunt
and sold itself to the most brutish man in town

I had a friend named Of Baile
de dance
and his sister tried to drown me

She's dead now
having been run off life's untenable road
with her babies in their funeral seats

When was paradise my telos wants to know how soon

I stir St. Germain Fernet Branca and rye
with an ice spoon and get fucked
with my eyes closed
from behind

Was this the sweet promise of the angels of the saints

Do not be good with me or I'll find your Eden
and open its medicine cabinets

with my dissolute nose
I'll lose the keys in your neighbor's bedroom
and wear your wife's clothes over
my day-long erection

because when I was young I grew away
from the sun

Now I'm a Gothic hag sucking
coke from the snouts of men
who find me monstrous

Let's talk about angels
I saw one just returned from jail with his gentleness
flung over the couch next to his money stacks

We didn't know each other anymore
and never had

We were standing beside our youths like babysitters
But the truth is I was the only one who'd ever had one

A beautiful curled petal of high-mindedness
that I one day pressed to the tip of a penis
and blew away

I'm brown and my whiteness is an opaque jelly
that allows me to enter countless assholes

Not that I construct my womanhood in non-being
Not that I mean for these mechanics of identification to function
in this poem to make me a feminist of color

This poem I mean my lyrical mythologizing of my
bucolic thus already mythic childhood
a form in command of itself no matter how

humiliating or ironic the content
faith is a theory of experience I've employed here

Here in my wet bottoms
Here in my nylon thong
Here in my best client's hands
Here in the memory of my flaccid ill-spent youth
Here in my lazy fractured womb of bathic love

Is my boyfriend Eli Ohm
of aquiline nose of Spanish rape
I remember him when I open my underwear drawer
and it smells like my mother

whose scent curdles me
Her Indian blood I love it in my milk
Black vanities she gave me in the morning

I got my ass kicked for kissing a saint
Because I do that

I take absolutely everything that wants me
and force feed it til it gags and pollulates
into a violent swarm
that hates me

My father said no wonder everyone in town says
you're a slut you are

How useless is pity
How useful blame

My girlfriend was named Ami Real
That's a very nasty girl you're being so sweet with

Yeah
I mean yeah

Bless her
Bless her with a thousand verses
Deliver them in the queen's own lace

Suck her pierced tongue
till it waters
till the Lilies in the church bloom

for her beautiful gang bangs
and her juvenile detention

That crystal meth summer of high locusts
when I took them to the government park
and we sunk against the slide

and had our new torpor to share
That was it that was all
An identity to get past an identity that I can only now

the subjectivity of which I can access only now
Only now that it's clear the contradictions will never
dissolve into a whole

Let me be this cyborg
with a bad bad libido
and it everywhere at once shooting lazer ribbons

PRESTIGE BEAUTY BRANDS

The Hispanic population is making less money
but buying more expensive skincare products than ever
Gold-tipped tinctures and cloudy bottles of serum
wisps of status shining amniotically through
One man's crotch line flows sidelong into a manicured hand
The money practically drips through her fingers after all
it is a serum when the mother sockets dry
Her skin has been revealed like never before
in the Bertolucci warmth of a D.F. night club
as she blots some dew from her brow
with the back of her wrist the glistening smear
of it highlighting her silken veins
One woman is far away and one is very near
and in the middle is a blur where our Hispanic Beauty
may one day come into focus
When she demurely put wrist to forehead to unsnarl
some cute thoughts
The focus group broke into an ecstatic mutual heat
as her escort reached for his wallet
It was working
Chapultapec Castle was reversing itself sequined and painted
like a drag queen Faust
Our Hispanic Beauty knows
we begin female and become empires
Staring off at the dark hills of paradigm the data plays
on her surveyed cheekbones
She looks so youthful she might as well have not been born
like those 14-year-old-boys
who once died at her breasts with the flags
wrapped around their shoulders
Somebody get our Hispanic Beauty an oppositional gaze
or at least a drink
Simone Weil naked save for leftist pamphlets
enters looking bruised as an evening eye shadow palette
Now in the movies / Now in a Fiscal Year Presentation

When the dopey husband in the Seven Year Itch goes
out for a chaste vegetarian meal
he's served by Weil and later
the first utopian-cum-racist scene is superimposed on
clips of the US Army snapping open her legs
and letting in their trade
In light of all these robust consumer insights
how will our Hispanic Beauty get her heels between
the eyes of the market

INTERVIEW

My lover kissed my sleeping face this morning
I stretched out my arms guileless when the door shut
Then I got a message: "I bet you have lots of stories to tell"
I felt wet because it was morning
but ad nauseum I'm tired of being an engine
My first ever lover messaged me right as my
current lover was leaving for work
Wow I am so straight who can get here first to fuck me
The structure of their absence is hefty it lies recumbent on top of me
I need to worry
Today I don't have a job
I am a white person a professional
a somewhat opaque but pleasant companion
Now I'm told that my beauty is timeless
which I take to mean that I don't look old
I value prudence after all I haven't had children or taken a stressful job
The past makes me feel romanced upon
it's an imposition and yet I'm obsessed
When Sophie Calle hired a man to stalk her it was for getting caught up
Divorce is ok I say as a child speaking
Not much has changed my vagina is 15 and it is baseball season
I open another window and look for deals on Botox in NYC
There's nothing for me in a playground
its art scene parts my hair only messily

OFF-DUTY MODEL

It's money time
Bar Pitti is awash in late afternoon dank
The sun is nuclear rubble on my wrist holding the menu askew
Sometimes life is too self-loving
In a big hat my brows are slugs
and I'm vexed by the cruelty of bees
Hum with me oh ye dead ingenues gone to Kansas full of blame
When I'm old I'll be free
When I'm horny I can't have sex because I am ovulating
When I'm on birth control I can't have sex because I am not horny
When I'm pregnant I can't have sex because I'm blown out
When I'm a mother I can't bear to live
When I can have sex anytime I want I am sex negative
When I can't have sex I am full of it
The director sought his virgin idea in plain waters like a fop
I will forgive anything of the man I love
for I am arranged like a snail: front-loaded
with antennae too supple for the big haul
Goofy dangerous national complex
I'm a big ole haul of a thing nevermind the stunned pupils
A smart woman is a stylish stalking foil
Cruel bees sucking all the life from the poor flowers
Step lightly minx the camera can't backpedal too fast

DEAD FROM LIKE

There's a woman I admire
Every time I see her do something indiscreet I die from like
Soon I will run away but I'll continue to follow her
How did I get to be the eunuch in the relationship
I never thought I'd be so lumpy in spirit
At the border some men will die over me in slobber
but not here where I am only a conscript
Safe space at what point does it act like a word
and cancel out what's inside

MIMOSA TREE

A voice is duplicitous
Mine sounds like a child's
I love my family inappropriately
We were all born together
mother father and six siblings
from my womb
Everyone's voice eventually matured except for mine
It's my own fault
Rescue me pink slipper tree I remember
I like to sit around and make out with people
which is unkempt
and every year my apartment gets smaller
and further away
Failure impediment split
No one has asked me to sign a contract
that is actually a drawing of a palm tree yet
Sisters and brothers I'm sorry
I guess everyone is going to fool me
until I get a big girl voice
until my thigh gets rubbed the right way
Fuzzy poms fall down

BLONDE ANTITHESIS

The kind of innocence that grabs you by the dick
and stabs you in the eye
Because all the best blondes have been brunettes
and learned the numerology of opposites
There is no blanche
There is only conspicuous absence of color
darker folds providing contrast
We were once witches
Then we were sensible and intelligent killjoys
Then they wanted to get away from us
in the arms of a toddler
So we became blondes
Blanche but you are you are
a cripple now
Everyone in Hollywood thought you'd be blonde
When you weren't they erased your legs
Scripts are for girls hey anyway
The women have all agreed to be included as well as subversive
Now all the witches on TV are blonde
Drop the "e" and bare the roots to become lovable stowaways
demonstrating a desire to shift to please
or is it some kind of slick protest
Please just let us be everything to you father world
Helen and Marguerite and Shulameth
fuckable baby real girls and war profiteeresses
Are you afraid of me? Will you murder?
Something very unsavory happened to create brunette blonds
something based entirely on desire
That's why I am so common and perfect
Everyone looks darker comparatively including me
In having it all I have shown you how to have it all
an Aztec princess in a white silk bustle
Sun pixels blooming into pop songs
Straw so sick sweet and good to chew
Full corn in the height of a marigold noon
Lemons in a bowl of bathing chicks
Urine in the blue wind

Please join me for I have changed
Colorism swatches
Joseph Smith's belles
Honeyed promises of bondage deliver my milk
with iodine copper and realness

WAR

We can't speak Spanish to our grandparents
Corina gave her a name like Kimberly crossed with Timothy
She threw a bag of crack rocks down it sounded like dice
Chinge le chinga le chinga le winge le
a coto moroto moroto man
This was in a mobile home at the entrance to a ranch road
where Tom was killed ending the 17th century of my Christian life
NAFTA is us oh hominy hominy hominy how many
boys are in the backyard with guns

STRAIGHT DUDES

Why are you
still here

NARCO CORRIDO

There's a dog in Maine who is known for his charisma

The waves sometimes take out your legs
as they carry you towards enlightenment
Ask Kate the woman who drove her minivan into the sea

and our priest who was on his way to live out
the rest of his life secretly with his lover in Laredo
when a Mexican cartel chopped him up
and buried him under his new house

The community thought they needed to help that two-legged dog
Then they discovered he was helping them

LYRIC DATA OR LUST

ache _says the purple sky

I scroll through pages_

never finished_ with this turgid non-tangible

desire is an embolism

in the_wake_ of health

I'm always saying_ desire like I'm a theorist

_like my mouth_is a mirror_caked with vaseline

_slid halfway _inside someone's ideals

clink goes the ice_

There's no_ vacation timeshare_

that can _contain_ my torpor

When I was an angel_I loved fucking_

_in the cottony spell_spinning in a

_ a sweetheart neck_rocking specious _baubles

Chilling_unstately_ yet so _like a mascot for

give it to me_harder_than_a

boulder
(_undeliverable_)

_harder_than_that even_

When I was_ _holy monogamous

_they called me Pix_But now

wiped clean_ they just prune

nevertheless _ _

I am DTF

THE FLIES

Shorn Semitic Solomon of mine hair
in your mouth of mine bitten skin of
actually yours
We are not brother and sister
though our breasts both point east
We fucked like jocks
because in the past we were
and already reproaching ourselves palms open
for an allegorical love beyond our control
avoided metaphors
Confession is the deepest structure
and has survived only as parody for 500 years
I'm the vengeful kind
In this way I am flea-bitten
and for the sake of literary kinship
I let myself be gnawed
I know I shouldn't
waste my time with the sacred
while my brother's life is opened by war
In a barn in Somalia
through his autoerotics I return to myself
My flesh is rosy as the morn
when throned on ocean's wave
and it passeth o'er
Death and his brother Sleep
One pale as yonder waning moon
The other is back where she started
Yet both so passing
by the other and through this brother
Jade asphyxiation of mine
His cream mine toothpaste
His cream mine eyelash adhesive
His mites my tragedy
abuzz with wonderful!

VIBRATOR

When you get a girlfriend I will really die
With me the world will rot
As it is it will be five years before we can go to the Poconos
10 more years will pass before I divorce my first husband
By then you will have erectile dysfunction and we'll be ruined
because your dick
Is my favorite part about you
Your dick and your eyes
I love your dick so much I could just cry I could just cry
Another woman said that to me about your dick
and I could see that she really wanted to cry
Tears were balancing in her eyes
clear like the color of my cum
You have already changed me
You may try to be breezy but I will be there
humidity pressing on your neck
You didn't expect me to be so hot
You didn't expect my vagina to be this hot
I am like a miasma seeping in
greater than radiation in another epoch
My magnetism once wicked the ocean dry
Now I carry vials of it inside me
where your dick sometimes sloshes
Where the memory of riptide must want to spill out
I have seen our failure but not yet made peace with it
Because I come from a place made of thorns and wetness
so I know you are in my bramble ensnared
But in the end it's your flesh that will injure me
Your perfect manners hurt me
when you order me a drink
When you order your dragnet a drink
You should call me that
Because I am a mechanism of conquest
That you later smash apart
See how the waves pound the sand and flee
after sopping it

I did not want to love you
because I am already dead
But that doesn't matter
A lot of people have said they love me anyway
They think of me now with awe and pity in their hearts
A man with an anchor tattoo on this train is not one of them
though someone with his forearms did follow my voice
through a carnival once
because I was a hundred lights flashing in a little girl's heel
and a squeaky horn on a pink bicycle

SKUNK HOUR

I am starting to have fun
Some people are on their honeymoons because they have salaries
paid vacations and sick days
Some people are squeezing out the afterbirth
in their hospital beds and feeling ok
Another way of saying I don't agree is saying I don't believe in it
My boyfriend is patting me on the back with strokes of conciliation
His phone is always buzzing with sexless missives
I don't believe in intentions in this neoliberal context
pitted binaries of male universality stroked by Uma Thurman's scream
I don't have an age just suspension and Millay
I would rather flirt with a hick than be a female lumpy space
How many times have you seen the word noble in front of intentions
That's the problem with intentions
They are bourgeois they are in English
and will drive you to drink
miles of millstones
Perhaps I cry because I can't believe
how much there is I don't believe in
Whatever I am please look later

AVIGNON

The evangelist's pamphlet
is the real face
I'm not embarrassed that I prayed
with my mouth rooting
in the grass and felt
that there was an understanding
absence-presence below me
hollow enough to fit my paltry personal paradoxes
That felt like Grace without the Word
A mute end in itself
like how it must have been
before Abraham started
hearing voices
Though I suppose the problem
was that he heard *one* voice not many
Logos came later
as a dom with a plastic rod
after centuries of being tied to the bed
I'm talking about a living sleep
uncreative and unrelated to death
Gnostic as this is I felt a little bit
of my life drop into it
Belly to belly with the snake
Nothing I really needed
but nothing I needed
to purge either
Part of the endless party that is
my leap of faith re: enlightenment
that seeks it in rational certainty
and elevated states
other people's sex-misery-joy apparatuses
or whatever cocktail gets you up
behind the podium of your first real age

The God underground
is uber-gravity
a sucking back in of the seed
If I were talking about immortality
I would be embarrassed
but I'm talking
about Simone Weil's suffering
after she didn't die in Spain

NOVELISTIC DISCOURSE

Forgive me, but all this time I have been addressing this audience in personal epiphanies, disfigured and alienated from social realities, that I disguise as theories or otherwise lazily put forth, intact and unwieldy, to be worked upon by the for-granted Marxism of neoliberal children longing for a humanism for which they can provide dutifully — like a father would have at some point in history (I forget who said this) until it's no longer grateful. Has anyone here been touched by the Father who writes poetry in the corridors of ruined manors? Anyone? No? I, for one, certainly have and will not forget the damp tilled rows beset in my manic waves of purple polyglot. Now, dear murderers, I've given you a clue. But perhaps you'd like it better if I called you...something else...

A question was raised.

Enter three characters in search of the difference between artifice and art (but really performance and its work) in the early 20th century — thinking especially of ruined women in puce hotel rooms. There are tassled curtains and tears everywhere.

They: Forlorn.
Me: Inflamed.

"Would that I were to take a lover tonight, he would be one for original phrases meant to describe axioms to which I have no claim, such as 'Jewish geography' or 'Goy thinking,' and yet somehow I would feel as if I have all the access in the Western world. For example, who taught me to write stage directions? No fucking one. And yet (waves handkerchief like a dinner bell). I've just thought of what to call you. Now please reply with your comment.

Of course your mother "Likes" you, her most handsome son. How like us to sit in the dark together and talk of Catholic princes in dresses with blue knuckles weighed with their Sea's worth in baubles when really, you and I, we're a little bit trashy and we know it. But honestly, I'd rather be. What's that — you say you're discovering a new discourse? No, honey, that's happening all the time. Well, every time we show up to an N+1 party and don't talk to anyone but each other. You're just slow enough that you notice. Now back to our truly bestial affair. Do it like we did in the old town before a vintage boutique in the West Village Instagrammed me with 40 hashtags, floating like so many sailboats carrying nothing. Your hands like that. Like a butch heiress in a wealthy country would do it.

Another question from the audience.

They: Jealous.
Me: Loving it.

Yes, I can easily say that as a white bourgeois presenting person who is not white bourgeois I can't afford activism because I am too busy working, have no safety net, wouldn't know how to go on were I unable to drive my uninsured truck to the nearest gas station to buy whatever beer is on sale, intimidate my children into silence, turn off every light in the house, crack one open and watch muscled pigs slaughter each other on the auction block of midlife. I do this with my father. Or else I dress in my grandmother's brooches and drink red gin in The Refinery Hotel. You look like something, but what? They all say that.

Family narratives obsessively constructed by people who despise their families. And Freud. And, haha, even people who despise Freud.

I made the available decision to live in a fairy tale. I pretend my labor isn't my real labor. I'm religious. I think language is powerful. It is. I don't do anything about it. I don't write like "today."

When I said sometimes language doesn't carry any information, I didn't mean that it wasn't a sign system created for the singular purpose of conveying information. Maybe I meant it doesn't carry meaning, which is like naïve, I guess. Or maybe I just meant I didn't like this Philip Roth novel because the girl character didn't make any sense. You could see how scrambled up he was about women, about people. Thus, these sentences failed as vessels of a unified experience. For me. I'm a girl. But perhaps also a genius?

They: Can you explain yourself?
Me. No, it's humiliating.

Back to the sex we were having. You grew astoundingly large in my mouth, but we had yet to have a Biblical encounter. A co-worker had advised me to get you to your finest moment and then pounce. That's where language made itself felt in the most lucid way. A fine moment. What organization and economy. It creates a little cloud for metaphor to live inside.

Helping people meet their own needs is ugly. They become monstrous with want. Everyone's Rousseau is in the audience tonight.

Enter four critics in search of a slim gay male author to claim as their prodigy. Emma intercepts them, knocking over a glass of cognac and tripping on her tote bag to grasp at their sleeves.

EMMA: Pay attention to me. I can write in so many different ways. An authentic inscription for each lover, so to speak. Plus, I can't help but become well-known in art circles because my life — it has been so interesting!

CRITIC 1: I can only tell you what I told your predecessor. Go out alone. Seek not a family or a community among those who will eventually efface you with their blob mentality.

EMMA: No, but you're wrong. A man wrote a story in which I am destroyed without taking into account that I might enjoy it. So here I am to enjoy it. Commedia D'ell Arte.

CRITICS 2,3,4: Woody Allen wrote for us to say we see someone we know.

EMMA: I packaged myself for you!

They: Stagnant.
Me: Redeemed.

The Return of the Story

One lover came furiously to the front of my mind as a man with very thin lips. I did what I wanted and failed at even that. When I was a child we would ride our bikes to see an old goat with gigantic balls. I wasn't amused. I would turn to watch a domestic conflict or meditate upon a cow-like family plopped in an open garage. Blind and pale bottom-feeders positioned outwards, expectantly, in folding metal chairs. Only later did I find that I preferred talking, instead, about the goat's balls. Remember when I forced you to imagine where I grew up?

For me, the rest of the story expands geographically, unfurling beyond the useful-ness of verbal construction or psychological deconstruction — beyond structures itself. At least, it seems that way when we're talking about something so pastoral. The motion of the bike is forward, the motion of my memory backwards. Then colli-sion. Then ricochet. Stop. Time and memory finally entwine their wires and crank me forward in a vision of space to the cemetery, where in the future (of this partic-ular past) I'd watch my first friend be buried. All this time I've resisted saying there was nothing else to do in that town. Poor white people and *poor* white people.

Q: When will they hate each other as much as they should.

A: When they meet.

Caveat: A lot of money will have to be burned.

Those evenings I waited in the back bedroom attached to the bar for you to come in and watch Lonesome Dove with me. Do you hate yourself, I asked. No, but what would your parents think of you being with a skin.

This has got to be some kind of movie!

I wrote that he had given me the best orgasm of my life, and later my boyfriend read it and told me he had seen something sad in my diary. Pointing to it, he looked very sad. There is no reason to be jealous, I said. He said that wasn't it; rather it was that I had written about receiving oral sex from a person who was now dead, whom I had loved. No, that's the wrong Tom, I said. The timeline is skewed. Please, I said. It's the end of my life and there's nowhere else for this to go. Listen as it rushes out.

I watched Barack Obama's first election in a bar without edges or boundaries. I loved a man who had watched his father, a businessman, sort women's apparel in the basement. That was his business. Confessing to me that he did not know whether he was affluent or not turned him, before my indignant eyes, into something like a plastic bride on top of a cake.

Leaving Beverly's, leaving Cafe Loup, leaving The Iroquois Hotel, leaving a pocket square, leaving pastures, leaving open waters, leaving two women in my bed, leaving mania, leaving my own name lit up in green glass — I often felt nothing like a desire for intimacy. Though I waited like a dog for his hand to reach mine and dreamed that, slipping on his cum, I fell on the sidewalk. My Aunt Florentina appeared and poured oils into my bath. Already, what a wild and wonderful sensation to feel this little one moving inside me. Can't wait to meet him or her. No, without milestones, what else is there but a gel of time. Taumalipas. McAllen. Laredo. Caught in a wrinkle.

A little girl with my last name fell into a drain. Be a ramp to your sisters. All the stores were closed the next morning, and we went out, you and she and I, into a circular Google, where each woman's question was the other's top hit. I've known a country without commerce. Ghosts feeding on cured meat. It's all about the libidinal relationship between objects, you know, like Katherine Mansfield. David Lynch. To a disappointing lover, dripping syrup from my jaw to the white, white petals of male intellect, I say this. I watched Barack Obama get elected a second time. He could be the child of A$AP Rocky and Lana del Rey, and he is. Angels made love with humans and made giants that made him. But all of them drowned in a great flood.

Dostoevsky. Novels. Adam dead in The Seine. Me floating next to him. Black Angus. Charolais. Some I wanted to feed, some I wanted to kill. We drowned out of a lack of will. You began to manage the bar when your uncle froze to death, drunk, at the back door. White people came in the summer. Hippie girls with perfect yoga bodies ran naked through the trailer every afternoon. We have to do something with all these mountains in your eyes, because they pull me up towards the most Buddhist, most Christian, most beautiful annihilation. And I was never a "leap of faith" kind of person before. I minded the cattle guards and never fell in. Every night I walked under Post Oak trees, its wings expanding over an acre of moon-pied grass. My lover turned off his lights and waited. A civilian in Afghanistan showed Ben his son's homework, which was left undisturbed on the table when the drone killed him instantly. As he recounted this, I blinked slowly into my dumbness and could only make out grey shades and the sound of tambourines. I'm still there, crouching, a headless gargoyle. She who is I thinks of the trajectory of her own homework and decides she's never learned anything new.

I climbed the ranks of patriarchy with Cheryl Sandberg and my friend's mom who marched in marches in the 70s.

No, actually, I didn't.
But I did find an academic voice.

And made out Weil and Jasper and Sartre on the rim of an oil tank. I'm attracted to the thinking of people who say things I already know. So I'm missing what's really happening, the way MM missed the revolution of theatre.

"I can barely spell my name, but I know my personality will make me successful."
- Cassie, 2008, St. Mary, Montana

Let's get paid. Let's get bought! Let's be ascetics, feeding on ourselves. I am literally on the fence. Filling one hole with wine and another with a soft cheese, the gentle lady kissed her daughter goodnight. The mother. That was the dangerous relationship. Achieving white womanhood, that was the truest thing we did together.

I still haven't figured out what the good love of a good man can do for my art besides everything.

Epilogue: The World Appalling Comes To Mind

I was working a PR event in Beverly Hills and had just been introduced to "the most important doctor in LA" and "the most talented young screenwriter in LA." After trying to figure out 1) If I was working, and therefore slightly cornered, and 2) hot enough to approach in front of their cohorts, they greeted me. I ignored the doctor and grinned stupidly at the writer.

What do you do?

I'm a writer too!

Aren't you in PR?

God, I was warned you LA people would be stupid!

Have you ever thought about acting?

We went to a bar. I had expected the theatricality contained in clean, plastic blocks and columns. Not even a cord was showing. Having never known the proscenium, only the physical and imaginary barrier of the camera lens, the fourth wall had always worn a condom here in Hollywood. No one was actually able to touch me.

Why don't you say a few lines? Say: I set you upon my lap.

The bar was rodeo themed. Texas? South Dakota? New Mexico? A mechanical bull enclosed in a gigantic iron pen, reminiscent of carousels, druggily bucked off women in short skirts. It moved with the slow vertigo and jagged retreats of a rabid animal. Everyone was remarkably sober, yet giddy. The other woman at our table was making a bow out of the complementary ream of cotton candy delivered to our table. I had made a limp thing that people ignored. But when she placed the bow upon her head everyone cheered and applauded. The doctor leaned in to me, still not touching me, and said, "She's an actress."

Desperate to draw them back towards me, I delivered the line:

I sate you upon my lap!

SECOND EPILOGUE: Monstrance

Luigi Pirandello grew up in a village called Chaos. He'd never been to a funeral when suddenly his entire family died in their sleep. With no one to organize a memorial, he saw their bodies carted off to a Sicilian cemetery and then set about making paper doll replications of them. He wrote tragedies, inking the words into outlines of what he hoped were his family members' bodily proportions. They rarely ever matched. But sometimes. An idealistic and philandering man fitted perfectly around the shape of his father's doll one day. The more patriarchal, the more easily a culture lends itself to farce.

Meanwhile, my career in Hollywood was taking an odd route. I was 38 years old. It only really showed in my thighs, which were airbrushed when possible. I remembered that Sarah Michelle Geller had dealt with the same problem and how it eventually became too much. I think that will happen to me soon. I was fortunate to have the right look for Victorian period pieces.

I feel ridiculous staring at the Roman coliseum like this. I feel ridiculous having sex with a gay man. I feel ridiculous getting sick at Versaille. I feel ridiculous when someone says of Michelangelo's pieta, "A mother is always young." I feel ridiculous looking at Milanese fashionistas. I feel ridiculous around art that I remember from slides. I feel ridiculous memorizing dates. I want to drink wine and eat biscuits. I saw some of the world and it looked like whatever I was wearing that day.

I swear to you, it's becoming so difficult not to be mentally ill. This is the tone of my generation. Or one of them. See how I meta. See how I grow past the limits of legibility.

I don't know who is more the author: Dostoevsky or Raskolnikov.

Neither one of them is a hero. They're open, never to be closed again by the discourse of one author. These oysters in front of me call for their own consciousness, so I bestow it upon them like always.

When will I ever really be allowed my madness? Other discourses come in and I apply them to objects within myself.

1) Liberal humanist
2) Egotistical artist
3) Magnanimous friend
4) Capable socialite

and so on...

Then, like always, the objects win their subjectivity and churn endlessly. This is why I have tried to use surfaces to create other surfaces rather than changing the conversation. If one creates a character from one's muck, I want to meet that character on her terms.

This is about monsters. Blind murderous rage runs parallel with disinterested truth-seeking. Books are splayed around me unbecomingly. I created a private language with no consequences. Within it there is no fact or falsity. It's an imitation. The way a child rolls her eyes impersonating the adults before she understands irony. Society has taught me to have no need for it. It's men like society that have made me this way. No, don't say another word. I won't hear it.

At the same time that I — here I am using whatever I the situation calls for — I pinned the snake of evil under my foot while kissing a ship, resulting in plague, capital gain and the triumph of positivism. Then, bafflingly, I demanded a church be built by a waterfall in my honor.

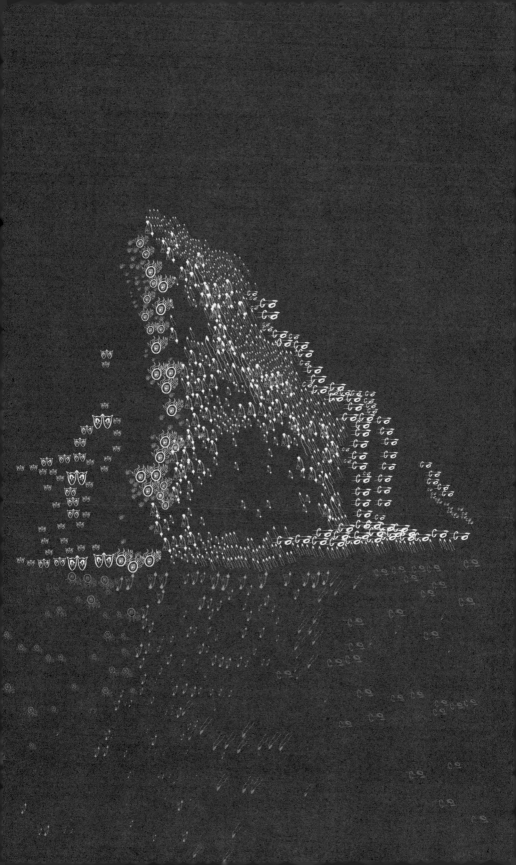

ACKNOWLEDGMENTS

Versions of many of the poems in this book have appeared in *Tin House, Jubilat, The Awl, Spork Press, Similar : Peaks ::, Composite Arts Magazine, Sink Review, Coconut Magazine, Brooklyn Poets, Glittermob Mag, Cosmonauts Journal, CultureStrike*, and the zine *Hologram.*

Several poems in this book were published in the chapbooks *Mood Swing* (Snacks Press, 2013) and *Mala* (Poor Claudia, 2014).

I would like to thank my editors, Sampson Starkweather and Justin Marks, for their generosity and patience; Emily Raw (interior design director), Mike Newton (interior graphic designer), and Eric Amling (cover designer) for creating the book of my dreams; the encouragement and council of Ben Fama, Rebekah McClure, Dorothea Lasky, Joyelle McSweeney, Kevin Killian, Brenda Shaughnessy, Craig Teicher, Todd J. Colby, Lara Glenum, Jennifer Tamayo, Jenny Zhang, Trisha Low, Niina Pollari, Madeleine Maillet, Jay Ritchie, and Menachem Kaiser; the memory of Tom Webb, Justin Murray, Brian Morgan and Adam Kittel; and the influence of my friend Ben Solomon.

This book is dedicated to Ben Fama, who sustains and inspires me.